THIS LONELY HOUSE

This Lonely House

John R. Milton

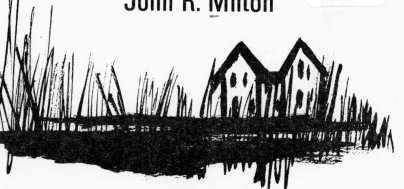

James D. Thueson, Publisher
Minneapolis

1968

Drawings by Lynn Milton

JAMES D. THUESON, Publisher
410 Groveland
Minneapolis, Minn. 55403

For Lynn, with love

CONTENTS

The Human Dream

Our Human Trust

Margindwellers

A Faulty Memory

Several of these poems were published previously by *Poet's Gallery, Chicago Review, Response,* and *Plainsong.*

the human dream

THIS LONELY HOUSE

The significance of this lonely house
Can readily be seen:
It entertains in silence the straggling weed,
And contemplates the human dream.

THE HISTORY OF MAN: TO DATE

I

An omnipresent spray of cosmic dust
Collides with green and earthy mists of spring;
From heatless rhythms of contextual space,
Planet-blown to gusts of fire-bred winds,

A thing is made, is shaped, is rudely born
Upon the likely brink of accident;
It sucks upon a warm and salty sea
And trembles with ambiguous destiny.

II

The amphibian awkwardly ambles then
Across the hot and new-won lava sands,
Dim-eyed looks back and does not recognize
The sea-arena, gray and hardly quit.

Unmindful of the fate which waits his touch,
He pauses for a moment, moves erect,
His brightening atoms stirred to vague commands
From restless energy of sea and sands.

III

A world to be explored, he takes his time;
Beneath the sun his consciousness expands,
Until in later life and other place
He senses first, then knows, that he is man.

With mind and voice of new identity
He thinks to speak with new and worn-out stars,
Squeaks dryly from beginnings in the dust,
Anticipates the rains, as long he must.

THE LANGUAGE OF GENESIS

Those bold beginnings still lie far
Beyond the aching human reach,
In words fleshed out so that rare deeds
May be believed, if only
For a moment more. To understand
Is once to take the logos shape and with it
Ease the breaking skin of our imagination;
A therapy perhaps, yet who of us endures
In only medium pain while tissues tense
And stretch across our unlikely bones.
Comfort remains a minor thing,
Never likely to redeem
At less than cost.

Our futile frame belies immortal blessings;
It withers in the finest sun
And dusts the place which we can never enter
Unless the name of it is uttered loud.
Language is our only life;
One word, first accidental in our world,
Provides the only grace.

A prophet's word it was, or was it then
A backward look to justify those moments
Out of comprehended time?
A poet's word it seemed to be, or was
The insight, tempered by rebellion, never won?
No matter now. Words are meant for newly-
Gentiled ears as well as ancient Jew,
And formlessness is hardly heard
Above the noiseless limitations
Of soft-textured flesh.

The shape of phantom origins held tight
Within the most ambiguous phrase
Is better than (and here we cry aloud!)
No shape, and not a phrase at all.

THE SHORT JOURNEY OF GAUNT JOHN

No foetus long remains aloof from signs
Of form; the open struggle of birth,
Subconscious yet, in fleshing red soft-
Tints a formal milk, the feed of anxious
Movement toward ungentle shaping ends;
And death awaits beyond
The constitution of a search. We go
In shaking egos on the legs of dawn,
To name a meaning and so delineate
Its kind.

        The shapes are there, fat-lurking
In amazement, meadowed, wooded, watered,
Aired in some resemblance to a fleeting thought;
And having thought, the foetal comforts
Burned away, two grasping breasts are thinly
Milked and water flows upon a wider world.

John drank this new-brewed poison and promptly
Died the common death. He joined
His people in the broadest restlessness
Of earth and sky. Grass-shot with questions,
Grown in sun, they groped through tiltillating
Nature, swallowed shapeless beauty, and
Retired in silence under leafless trees.

Consider:
        Gaunt John wonders where to go.
The clearest answer is, he must.
Stasis is the surest kind of death —
Annihilation by default. The journey
Is the thing, through burning bogs eleven
Times a major trap, with Adam standing coolly
On the other side, the first John, or William
The First, a decoy back to where it all began.
The world's a puzzle, the sun a false
Illumination casting shadows over bending grass
And making trees a spider-web across the ground.

Again, consider:
Gaunt John lies down
Upon his fleeting shadow, pins it to the earth
And presses without strength, until in death
He enters dusty wombs.
Journey is the shape,
Gaunt John, no matter short or long, and, O,
The form gives way to further form.

THE POET'S WORK

We name a name
And say the abstract word,
The word made flesh.
Humble eagerness
Derives from sensual pride,
And God in the orchard
Sits on his favorite tree.

We breathe a sigh,
Perceive persistent objects there.
Flesh, while only flesh,
Glows latently without an edge
Or shine; the clear-washed eye
Brings brighter agitation.

We speak a sound
Reverberating in the dust.
To dust it shall return
Unless blown clear by virgin winds;
A thing is molded then,
Emerging fitfully
To claim a further word.

We sing, as prophet
And the poet chant a new-found love
Across the black of space,
And wash it grey.

No other can we do,
Nor can a thing be better known
Until the god behind the word for god
Vacates the fruit-filled tree.

A PAINTING

A painting
hangs
upon the wall,

Creator's mind
or being
revealed for all,

Experience,
vague up to this time,
objectified

As once before
the same
was deified.

INTIMATIONS OF NON-BEING

A hawk floats in these high blue hills,
Upheld by arrogance and skill to touch
The sun and slide the slopes of air.
I am merely human, watching from below
With no goodwill, no art, no craft;
Nothing lets me hope to glide
In competition with this bird.

To be a flying man, to skip
The piercing trees, to skim with
Jauntiness the flinty cliffs and climb
Those gauzy chutes of space
To no dimension — wish upon a hawk.

No answer here but strain with metal
Bright upon its hammered pinions,
And chart a course from deep inside
The best machine yet made.
Not enough — the tragedy is swift —
For if I dip to possess my ridge
The hawk drops down in disputation,
Strikes past the ego'd eye suffering
In the sun —

       and I am unhooked
From ridge, from rock, from mountain side,
And from a dream no man can twice mistake
Except in high blue hills.

AUTO TRIP TO MOUNT EVANS

Above this lake the awkward summit path,
In jumping convolutions, carries us
Absurdly high above the dwindling plains.
We climb with painful hesitation, look
Beyond the dropping cliffs, and sweat with pride.
Wet egos, cold and slippery from ascent
To heights long glorified but not attained,
Laugh childishly and push us past the curve,
Past wind-stripped trees grotesque in lovely death.

We see our own death in mock serenity:
Like glacial rocks quick-tumbled to the depths,
Our bodies lie in stillness, nicely crushed
And lost beneath the ineffectual pines,
Removed in permanence from man's mad climb.
This is a tempting, satisfying end
For abstract minds, to turn the wheel and plunge
To peaceful coexistence with the rocks.

The dream is brief; our trembling hands restore
The neutral auto to its course, and place
Our destiny upon a further curve.

SQUAW PASS

High on the pass
the sky comes to an edge,
cuts cruelly deep
then skips upon a ledge
and in its course
begins a valley-dropping glide
that stops the breath
and seems to end in suicide.

A SUMMER NIGHT'S DREAM

The heat of summer wantonly embraced
my window;
only the fluttering moth
could walk across the glass,
touching lightly
with its fingered feet.

Evil sat outside upon the grass,
or so it seemed.
The only serpent was a pattern
in the window pane,
elusive, winding sideways
with a little forward hump.

Prior to a later rain
the movement had no motion,
because the wave was dumb.

A dream remains
for winter months ahead.
Memory works around
a sultry consciousness
that failed to bloom.

COMPOSITION AT MIDNIGHT

Once, alone, within the expanding confines
Of a midnight shade, all else
Asleep, suspended loosely
In the various dreams of death,
I woke to images of worth;
Elusive details settled in demand
Upon the dew-dampened ground,
Took seed in sunless soil
For the growth I hardly dared to know.
Perceptions placed apart
From mumbling crowds drew blood
And muscle from an unmarked place,
Sucked with parasitic strength
And swelled to childhood
In a moment never understood.

Now the question hangs,
Like a new-born chick stumbling surely
Within the shadow of its first and frenzied hawk;
Some inner language, lacking voice, speaks
And draws it back in mindless non-assertions
To evolve to further breath.
And I, alone in loving terror,
Wait through the after-birth of night,
Also afraid to meet the dawn.

THE PRIMITIVE

He saw the pools above the shore, blue-green
Among the rocks at first, then yellowed spots
Unused and foul from separation. Seen
Close, away from the sky and lake, the clots
Are scalpel-cut, as though to pare and clean
The mask of purity before it rots.

His mind of reason contemplates the pools;
He shrugs from him the beauty as too strange
For adoration save by neighboring fools.
He turns to worship where perceptions range
For sea-long distance, there where vision cools
And heals the soul with tide-renewing change.

He will not sit baptized in pools cast up,
Discarded, sick, and dying on the shore,
When there within his reach the holy cup
Itself stands primitive, pure as before.

A VIEW

above
below
we always know
that both are so

a black bird
leaves a dark trail
high
in the illusory sky

a white skull
gleams in the sun
and remains
firm in the dust-yellow plains

one tries
one dies
one always sees
dichotomies

our human trust

AND SO WE LOVED

And so we loved, from our necessity, we thought,
To join the rhythms of the stars. Then passion
Of embrace drew down the shade until we smiled
Within a starless night, and blood and breath alone
Survived.
        It is enough, we said, and hid beneath
The white-tipped waves of pulse. Great vows
Forgotten then, and moons effaced by thoughtless
Action toward no end, we loved in vain.

                    While
Stars fled west, dissolved, their rhythms shattered
By the shine of day, we broke, an error heated
By the sun. Sick, scorched by light, we ceased to love,
And lay through fevers of the healing years,
Forgetting stars but learning how to love.

And so we loved.
        Not from old urgency,
We knew, to melt our flesh to cosmic dust,
But in the freshness of the earth we loved,
In consolation of our human trust.

THE LANGUAGES OF LOVE

She said to me, or so it seemed:
No words are needed now,
Our love is but an action
Deeded to a final yesterday;
There is no concept,
Syntax has another task
And we should let it formalize
Around the subject of its choice —
No meddlers here within our state of grace.

Grace? my answer rose
In quest of something we had never shared.
A hand had touched me
Where response was quick,
A lip had quenched my speech
And sucked our conversations dry
Before they reached the air between us then.

Were words in need,
This were the angry time
When fleshed-out symbols
Might disgrace the deed.
What part of love survives
The composition of its act?
And having put the question, I must wait,
Because she cannot speak.

YOU WONDER WHY

You wonder why I love you less
At dawn. The moon has dropped away
To grace another landscape, dress
Trees unknown to us in pale grey,
And prompt a stranger to confess
In solitude his lady's way.

What touches us at dawn is not
The emptiness which follows love;
Nor have we soon, in light, forgot
The furry anguish screaming above
What seemed to be and yet was not;
Nor have the eagles killed their dove.

We learn at dawn, you more than I,
That all things rest before their birth:
The hawk relinquishes his sky
And sinks with sparrows toward the earth.
My love is then a morning cry
In recognition of its worth.

TO PROVE A MYTH

Where is love
When yellow rains wash angrily upon cold streets?
When tattered leaves
Quick-split from their ineffectual stems
Hurl down a curse and follow it to ground?
When frenzied feet in wet black boots
Beat stumbling rhythms deep in grabbing mud?
Green-heavy sky sits passion down,
And lovers run apart within this late spring storm.

Were Aristophanes upon this scene,
Symposium speeches hanging thickly in the air,
He'd likely have no answer to our failing love,
Might even fall his face to dirtied earth
And wish Hermaphrodite floating by in gutters
Choked with twigs.
Our myth belongs to Zeus:
May we rehearse it as before? Man unfulfilled
Since cut in two by careless rage, once halved,
And therefore not to have his love alone
But destined on the streets
As in the woods to mind his pain,
To bind his wound in marriage gowns
While reconstructing egos bent before his time
And antiquated by the several mournful myths.

Yet two and two are here:
The harried earth and wetting sky;
Thunder spoused by crackling domestic light;
A pair of frightened squirrels branched on high;
And, in the end, a dying day conceding to its night.

And you and I, umbrellas tilted up,
Eyes closed to rain and ears packed in with wind,
Upon this street-arena blindly we charge
Against the structure of our spoken plot.

Our panic dissolves in rain,
The ancient incompletion touched by pain
Of accident and long-awaited growth,
As Zeus again denies his legendary oath.

TO NANCI, LYING IN ICE PACKS

Child,
In you I see the likeness,
Uncomfortable, of me.

We fear the world
As early elms must fear
The gusty winds,

And the fires of spring
Upon the heels
Of disconcerting cold.

We sway
And bend too far at times,
Then catch up short

With the fevered breath
Of undue
Sensitivity.

We struggle,
Though we cry
In kinds of pain,

And my tears
Are selfish,
Because I am you.

THE GROWN-UP

Come, she said (young),
And walk with me beside the brook
Whose ripple-tips dart and slide
In unconsidered recklessness.
We walk, until the little rapids also tire
And fall from open sunlight
To my favorite midnight pool.
There, under trees mature
From silence of their guarded years,
We speak of smallish things.
Dark with Privacy not often
Toned by less than love,
Cool froth just-fallen from the upper stream
Slips down innocently one last time.
We watch it atop the pool,
Like milk in coffee cups
Absorbed in new identity
Before the first and hesitating sip.
She hardly waits
For my indecisive taste,
Assuring me the brook will hiss and laugh
Until we bid it stop.
I see the quiet pool again,
Wondering if its depths are measured
By nostalgia garnered in all previous
Waters rushing past, their course
but lightly obstacled until of late.
She sings, and runs along her brook,
While in the deepening darkness
I can only rest, and wait.

RUNNING BEAR AT THE MISSOURI

1800

He once agreed
to wait upon

the ancient rock,
the gray flat stone
fleck-stained in green;

The hawk flashed down,
a sign to touch
his soul alone,
no other one
receptive there,
and boy beheld
the man, as though
reflection in
a stream turned clean
between the slime
gave back not what
was there but what
he sighed for then —
the honors of
a fledgling chief.

1823

Again he dreamed
upon the rock;
false visions fell
like milkweed pods
when blown in times
of wind and war.

No spirits these
but mortal creatures
pale of eye,
determined to
encroach;
   black deeds
left sorrow there,
and honors fled
upon the hawk.

1878

Once more he waits
(the magic Three,
the white man said
religiously);

The land is red
beneath the plow,
and by the stone
all color's gone
but copper face
and green, still green
the river slime.

WESTERN GRANDFATHERS

I saw them standing there,
As in a vision whited
By the dry bleached bones
Of their careless past, these
Sad-faced grandfathers
On a sun-scoured western beach.
Anachronismic patterns
Played along the neutral sands,
Washed a tided meaning far
Upon the well-worn shore, to
Tickle nervously between old toes
And stir impossibilities
To life once more.

This shore is but the end,
And who began it all, or why,
Is long forgot before the simple fact
Of foolish courage: footed
Or on horse, they dared the plains
And laughed at desert dangers
While they died, or, later,
Drove their dusty wagons
Canvas-flapping into mountains
Not yet carved and grooved
For lookers at the land.

A rough geometry of earth
Claimed more than we can whisper well:
The cry to Mother Earth sprang
Desperately from aborigine throats
New-parched by daily apathy,
Their spirits unreliable at last
To share the deed; snaking river veins
Ran dry beneath the tourniquets of chance;
The swell in Mother's belly then
Was not fertility but bloat

In each imaginary fear; pale bones
Protruded through transparent skin
Once rich in grass;
Sweet breasts, as Tetons the lure
For bastard mountain men, quick-dried
To hump the wagons, breaking old
Determination into fragments sliding
Down an eastern slope toward homes
Abandoned in an earlier greed;
Until at last the Mother-corpse decayed
To gulleys, washes, sharp ravines
And broken ridges,
The eternal stink of buffalo
Herded wantonly with legs in air
Across the dead-red plains.

One set of children saw
Their copper fathers gently hoisted
On to platforms holy in the years before;
Now bodies drank of earth
And sky indifferently
Through pores no longer wet from use.
Oh Mother Earth, whose children
Played with horse and lance,
Bequeath — they said — one wisdom
Of the land: allow the white-skinned heroes,
Lately entered here, one soft
Concluding song,
Nostalgic, if it must be so, or bless
The end with one beginning more.

And, done, it made no difference,
Except the stretching of a tenuous time
One generation closer to its death —
These unspecific shores.
These pale fathers, widely bred —

Unhorsed, they stood uneasy by the waves
Of history, squirmed in rhythms of returned
Events, and looked with awkward grace
For sons. I saw them standing there,
And fretted while they died again.

TO A FRIEND WHO HAS LOST HIS WIFE

Fearful lest my joy should fade
And I be left alone, I hurried
Toward the end of day. I threw
A stone in front of stretching shade,
And flung a backward glance
To stop the sun in flight.
It was no use. The day had gone;
My deer had ceased to prance
About the mountain wood, and love,
The one from yesterday, had run
Ahead of me and found the night.
Could I assume that like the sun
And sleeping hawk my love
Would quicken in the early morning dew,
Then all is easy with the rhythms
Of our daily dance. Yet we renew,
By rising to an individual dawn,
The bird and tree that linger
In receptive hearts, and minds,
Long after the flower has gone.

DRIFTING

Surf pounds commandingly
upon the beach, yet leaves no mark.
Cold eagerness is spent, and coiled,
and spent again. Impressive sea,
it moves for nothing but to grasp
and carry driftwood on its flanks,
to harry ships and reasonable men.
And, having done, it moves away
to wash a passive shore.

I drift as well upon the fluff
and foam until my discontent
turns eyes beneath the surf.
I stop the course of floating wood,
take note of what debris can do
to innocence of mind, and with alarm
dive deep, like Ibsen's duck
escape it all.

Then down beneath the tides
and shifting winds, where panaceas
wait and mysteries lure the unofficial
soul, I swallow salt. Indignation burns
the last resource; life there is drifting too
and nothing knows its end.
I fail passion, and forfeit reason,
swinging with the tides until the seasons
on the surface leave their mark.

margindwellers

CHICAGO WEST: NOTES FROM THE TRAIN

I

The NP train is a green worm
    coming out
        of its hole in Chicago.

The womb is dirty, and the birth abrupt.
Chlorophyll was discovered somewhere else.

II

We have left the Mother,
    oh sooty parent
        soon to be denied.

Birthsac shaken from head and feet,
flung wetly at the platform crowd,
caught by St. Christopher perhaps.

III

First sign of life is emptiness,
the unused trains in parkformation;
a gutted factory with its product lost,
brittle skin of bricks,
wood and metal guts that bounced and splashed
around
as discontained intestines are likely to,
and all for progress;
trucks of apish red backed up to view
like jungle apes confined to city zoo.

IV

In every station people stand along the westward
track,
blurs of fabric color,
blobs of fleshy dolor,
dead and deadly on the platform made of rusted
iron,
waiting, waiting, expectantly —
in each substation are they waiting for Godot?

V

Coal cars rumble past us toward Chicago
to feed a multitude of city fires,
return with cinderheaps burned out and dead

(while somewhere out ahead upon the prairie
bison chips were used not long ago as fuel,
the bitter cycle of eternal life
reluctant to conclude
in cinders and in smoke)

VI

Tenements, unlikely in the heavy air
along the L,
suspended porches screened
from nothing.

Are there ladies in these flats?
Round ladies in these flats?
A thought, a guess, and bedrooms have receded
as to space and time mis-deeded by some
careless realtor.

VII

Margindwellers trapped in brick and stone;
fourplexes staidly laid between the lumber yards
and pharmacies;
here by a sandy ballpark
blue-dressed cubscouts
shuck their bat and ball
and troop along behind a man: he's fat,
he's middle-aged,
he smokes a large cigar
which burns away to distances established by the train.

VIII

A blond and shorted giant on an English racing bike,
a fancy office shouting real estate and not so real,
gardens without flowers and the vegetables in cans,
bungalows all in a row (it's nice they can),
a mess of pottage houses many sizes fewer shapes,
a pretty sign with blue and white says "Bicha Furs"
and may be right,
a pair of towers full of water yet to drink,
a curving slanting rhythmic asphalt street,
and a pond with paper floating on its rhythm

a water tank	a lumber yard
a real estate	a local bard
a house of brick	and a house of wood
a one-floor house	where a two-floor stood
a short back yard	without a fence
and a two-tone Buick	full of dents

IX

She told me that her children were good travelers
Then she spent the evening beating them
I should have asked the children how their mother traveled

X

And when will Chicago stop?
How long shall it run
                and grasp with greed
toward prairies shining in a purer sun?
                Do we really need
the cityplace, the crowdplace, the peopleplace,
and the octopus who stretches tentacles beyond the bounds
of reason?
Here comes Chicago. And so we run.

XI

South of Winona Junction

                              an image

A heron flying down a dim wet alley

                              ungainly

Curving off and dissolving

                          in the trees

I don't know where the heron went

                             no matter

He left his image

                     for anyone to use.

XII

Somewhere . . . . far out
we know that this will stop

                       or

better yet it

                 will have stopped

when we arrive
at prairie towns where trains speed in and out
those towns with edges sharpened by the stalks of
corn and wheat
and all within divorced by county lines
and silent grass is noisy only in the wind
and one hears whispers from the grass when all alone
until the screaming winds

        afford another

          isolation

in the center of the gusting blast
and sometimes men go mad while man and town exist alone
and yet some men survive

        sufficient

         like the town

uncomplex in terms of brownbrick progress down the track

XIII
He said (in beatnik style)
talking as usual about the road
that it stood in symbol fashion
for the greener pasture hopes of men
        so then
        I looked from my window at the day's road
        and asked him where everyone was.

XIV
The city calls, eight hundred miles down the track,
the city pulls,
the multitunneled dungeon of the world with its own hot winds,
it sucks and howls against the train

XV
Chicago sucks in thunder on the little prairie folk
        but wind-blown grasses call
        where cowchips can be burned
        to make some sense
        and incense too.

A BRIEF PITY FOR LOVERS

Here, tree limbs reach
like soon-reluctant lovers' arms,
rustled apart by wind
and especially the whimsy of winds.

There, lovers in the city
below this suburbanized hill,
are a crowd-nestled pair
split briefly toward a longer
unseen death.

Alone, they might yet live,
unpricked by all the rest of us,
untouched by human densities
or brushed by clusters
of worm-holed leaves
clashing in the common wind.

SERENE AT SEVENTEEN

Serene
In her virginity
At seventeen,

Her life a darkness
Of peace,
She dared not bloom

In spring
Nor fulfill her promise,
Dismal this year.

Too much animal
She thought;
Then, once, condemnation

Dulled her mind,
And the puritan slept
With forbidden dreams

Until the darkness
Burst
Of its dark emotions.

In the splendor
Of new-found flesh,
Though pondered briefly,

She transcended
Daily devotions in the buds
Of rebirth.

AN EXISTENTIAL CHOICE

If only I could press my breast,
She said,
Against the bark of pines, and
So bled
Of once-imagined milk not shared
Re-run
My race of false emotions and
Be done.

Needled by her neutral pines, she
Drew back
Upon herself and spared her breast
Its rack
Of natural touch, to keep it soft
And white
And inauthentic for another
Night.

MR. PRITCHARD AND I

From faded roses, petals fall
but once; and I have stood aside
and watched the flower die.

In every alley, leaves are brown
and crisp; and I have trampeled them
to dust the town nearby.

Our Mr. Pritchard curses god
today; and I am home, ashamed
to know he found the lie.

DOLDRUMS

Dullness, at this present time,
Comes too quickly, as it could
Even to the less sublime
Hidden weakly in the wood.

Sunshine spears its way to me
Often, as a light of mind;
This is how it ought to be,
Not the darkness I now find

Cloaking me like all the rest.
Now dullness makes us brothers,
Fading sun slips off my breast,
Farewells me, like the others.

a faulty memory

SECOND WINTER DAY

The cut of northern wind leaves scars
Unnoticed for a day or two. Concern
Will softly fade by an orange fire,
And blue enamel sky can be dismissed
By intervention of a papered wall.
One wonders then about the cold:
Are consequences only fragments
Of projected fear, to be forgotten
In the woolen itch of heavy wraps?
What matters it that someone's ancient man
(Grandparent, it was said in whispered hush)
Froze fleetingly beyond the fire
And ice-preserved his soul
Before our time, and his?

We've conquered nature now:
Insulated houses squat with inner brightness
Like sun-filled caves, correct and safe.
But we must linger out beyond the line,
Build snowmen, castles, and skating rinks
From heavy water and a little innocence.
The frost takes subtle bites;
A wolf howls anxiously upon the plains;
Our sun grows dim, and nature,
Now defied, throws off benevolence
With irritating ease.

The winds of winter wait a day or two
While scars itch healingly on surface skin
And terror digs deep passages
To gouge the soul and fester sweetly
In the next unguarded winter day.
Our sin is but a faulty memory,
And death will always seem unfair.

A KIND OF EGOISM

trees
      sparsely
            spaced
on a hillside
place
      patterns
            treelike
in lace network
I
      see
            softly
through the laces
and
      walk
            warily
through the trees
and
      pity
            people
who become entangled

EVENING INDISCRETION

(In a Denver apartment)

A radio thickly fills my universe
With sounds redundant and intent confused,
Glowing tubes call up a blackening curse
Upon machines incontinently used:
While off in the valley, wind whispers in trees.

Upstairs the plumbing, sympathetic
To all din, resounds in gushing chords,
A menace in ceramic caves, frenetic
In convenience which it affords:
And up in the mountains, wind speaks to the trees.

Around me wondrous howling creatures, crib-
Confined and not yet taken with this world,
Awake at night-odd times, rehearse ad-lib.
Unmindful of the challenge they have hurled:
And down by the river, wind sings in the trees.

With slamming doors and hall-resounding feet
And other evils more or less like these,
I find it increasingly indiscreet
To remember the rustling of leaves on trees.

TOO LATE THE SUN WENT DOWN

Too late the sun went down —
I had already seen this day up close,
As though a microscope had tunneled me
Without advantage, and my hope
Had slid the tube and found a moral germ.

Neighbors have identified a psychic sin —
The closing of both eyes, or blinking
On a world better hid by dark.
Involvement is the current plea,
And loneliness must beg in vain
A private sea.

MEMORY IN BROWN

I'm too young
to remember
sleek brown ponies

fretting, cavorting
under copper-brown
riders and

dumb-lapping
the Missouri of
its muddy brown water.

It happened,
this I know;
I see no tracks,

yet brown —
a color often dead
from dust of land

and heat of leaf
in autumn sun —
may also be

nostalgic
and so a part
of me.

THE PUMA AND THE HUNTER

Slowly slowly the puma passes,
Death riding deep inside
Where chaos swells to strain its limits
And leak through the tawny hide.

Disdaining to recognize his fate,
He pads the yielding earth
With falsely summoned strength, and listens,
And sniffs, to find its worth.

Futile gestures for a thing near-dead,
Foolish to run the flood,
Yet cruelly pleasant (smell the hunter!)
To drown in its own blood.

THE SAME BLUE HERON

The same blue heron stood for a while
on the shallow edge of the River James
five late afternoons. A twisted mile
away her nest did not yet bear names.

Walking across the marsh, I could have found
the place and returned within an hour,
unless I paused by the burial mound
to bring those aging ghosts a fresh white flower.

The heron knew her river well, I think,
having pegged it with her spindly legs
like a tent, anchored in the purple pink
of sunset water, a drink whose dregs

came floating new each day, wanton and fresh.
No age was listed there, and knowledge came
unlearned from the primitive mesh
of memory, no easy source, and no easy name.

Her leg, a pointer, stirred in the flux of sand
and fixed our moment together. Forgetting the nest,
and holding the river loose-cupped in my hand,
I let the heron answer to my tardy quest.

ONLY THE HUNTER IS SHAPELESS

The slough was soon afloat with birds, blown in
By winds from distant places, gathered from the grass
Too stubbled now to undulate like waves.
Intuition guided them across the waste, riding breezes
Past the geometric lines of wire and post.
No hunter, I, the fact of flight impressed me more
Than rudenesses of death, and softly watched
The wrinkled waterway disturbed but lightly
By the bobbing birds. Ripples marked a brief identity,
A visual life, vivid in its form
But short enough to make it sad.
Tomorrow, the shapeless huntsman.

A LOCALISM — NORTH

One asks why elm trees grow this well
When oak does not and maple not
At all. Fat answers float on clouds
Across a field of blue; clearly,
Says the analytic mind,
This tree needs this, and that one that,
Rainfall measured in the choice, and
Quality of earth. Quick frost cuts
Down ambition; the rings of growth
Turn whitely inward, choking on
Thin sweetened sap whose flow is drawn
In suicide to starving roots.

Ah, regional, you say, and plant
The proper bush for shorter days,
Trimming maple branches from the
Reach of wind, and shrugging, digging,
At the spaded womb for one more elm.

But this is reason, and the poet
Cries reluctantly upon his bed
Of fresh-cut grass, proposing
Softly that a tree is like a soul,
Growing as intended and strangely
Sheltered from the inquiring mind.

MEMORIAM: FORT ABRAHAM LINCOLN, DAKOTA

This is a lonely place.
The belly-hackles rise
Up quick, premonition
That we know this grassy
Plain, the river flowing
Brown in mud, made blue by
Passing love. Though once it
Bid a last farewell, the
Ridge possesses us for
Moments of renewal.

We know this place, of course.
We too, past Custer's time,
Have dripped our blood as well
Upon green-growing sod,
Have learned that war and land
Strike deep, inseparably,
Upon the swelling soul.

This is a lonely place,
Except for brotherhood
Of blood and dust, memory
Dispersed beneath the moon
And crumbled in the sun.

TERMINATION OF THE HUNT

Smoke no longer curled
above the crested trees.

Dead,
I said

and ran up the ridge
that blocked me from his death.

Aspen leaves dried yellow
in the yellow October sun;

frost chilled my mind
and fear shook my legs;

a hawk fell low to push
his talon into rabbit fluff.

Death sat at ease, and
the mountains held aloof;

the sorrow was all mine
to drip upon the flowered tracks

of aimless deer,
as I tripped on rocks

blood-red in my imagination.
Then I saw him,

lying neatly in the symmetry
of death, ashes

from his fire cold in time
and pleading for a logic

that the man forgot
or never had a chance to learn.

No matter what the accident had been,
I felt no further

than the beating of my winded heart,
or lung,

to find the melody
in what was lately sung.